STEEPING IN HISTORY

A LOOK AT INDIA'S ICONIC TEA CULTURE

DR. JAGADEESH PILLAI

|| Dedicated to all wisdom seekers around the World ||

Contents

Contents

Prayer

"Om Bhadram Karnebhih Shrunuyaama DevaahBhadram Pashyemaakshabhiryajatraah SthirairangaistushtuvaamsastanoobhihVyashema Devahitam YadaayuhSwasti Na Indro VridhashravaahSwasti Nah Pooshaa VishwavedaahSwasti Nastaarkshyo ArishtanemihSwasti No Brihaspatir DadhaatuOm Shantih, Shantih, Shantih"

The literal meaning of this mantra is: OM. O Gods! Let us hear auspicious words from our ears. O reverent Gods! Let us behold propitious visions from our eyes, let our organs and body be stable, healthy, and strong. Let us do that which is pleasing to the gods in the life span allotted to us. May Indra, inscribed in the scriptures, bring us fortune! May Pushan, the knower of the world, grant us prosperity! May Trakshya, who vanquishes enemies, bestow us with blessings! May Brihaspati bring us success!
OM Peace, Peace, Peace.

About The Author

Dr. Jagadeesh Pillai is a renowned Guinness World Record holder, writer, and researcher hailing from Varanasi, also known as the abode of Lord Shiva. With a Ph.D. in Vedic Science and a range of creative ideas and achievements, he is a true polymath. He is the author of more than 100 books including Research Publications. Although his roots can be traced back to Kerala, the people of Varanasi hold him in high regard and affectionately consider him one of their own.

In 1998, Dr. Pillai was offered a job at Banaras Hindu University, but he left the position after only two months to pursue greater goals in life. He believed that in order to study Indian scriptures and engage in other creative endeavours, he needed to retire from the daily grind of working solely for money at a young age.

He started an export business from scratch, using the knowledge he had gained from a previous job in the industry. His intelligence and unique approach to business led to great success in a short period of time, earning him more in just a decade and a half than he would have in a lifetime working in a government job. Upon the passing of Dr. APJ Abdul Kalam, Dr. Pillai decided to leave the business and dedicate himself to reading, studying, researching, and experimenting.

During his tenure in the export business, Dr. Pillai traveled to over 16 countries, gaining valuable insight and experiencing the world and life in detail.

Dr. Pillai has achieved four Guinness World Records in the following subjects:

"Script to Screen" - In this record, Dr. Pillai produced and directed an animation film within the shortest time possible, breaking the previous record set by Canadians. He has also received numerous national and international awards and recognitions for this achievement.

Longest Line of Postcards - For this record, Dr. Pillai created a line of 16,300 postcards on the occasion of the 163rd anniversary of Indian Postal Day. The event also included a questionnaire about the Indian flag.

Largest Poster Awareness Campaign - Dr. Pillai designed an awareness campaign on the subject of "Beti Bachao - Beti Padhao" (Save the Girl Child - Educate the Girl Child) to achieve this record.

Largest Envelope - In tribute to the Indian Prime Minister's "Make in India" initiative, Dr. Pillai created a 4000 square meter envelope using waste paper to achieve this record.

Attempted - **70000 Candles on a 210 kg Cake** - To celebrate the 70th Indian Independence Day, Dr. Pillai attempted to light 70,000 candles on a 210 kg cake, which was recorded in World Records India.

Attempted - **Documentary on Dhamek Stupa of Sarnath in 17 Languages** - Dr. Pillai attempted to create a documentary on the Dhamek Stupa of Sarnath, dubbing it in 17 different languages. The result of this attempt is currently awaiting confirmation from the Guinness World Records.

Dr. Pillai is skilled in teaching the Bhagavad Gita, a Hindu scripture, and is popular among young people. He has helped many young people improve their lives through his motivational teachings.

In addition to teaching, he has composed and sung numerous Sanskrit Bhajans and patriotic songs.

He has also written and directed several short films and documentaries for awareness campaigns, and has volunteered with the police in both UP and Kerala to spread awareness about various issues through videos and photography.

Incredibly, he has produced and directed over 100 documentaries about the city of Varanasi, all on his own.

He has also helped and guided more than 25 boys and girls to achieve world records through creative and innovative methods. He is a multifaceted person who uses his intellect and the blessings given to him by God to excel in various areas. He is both a teacher and a student, always learning and teaching, and is able to master any subject he comes across.

He is a selfless social activist and motivational speaker who has overcome struggles and failures to become a successful and enthusiastic individual with a rich life experience.

In addition to his work with the Bhagavad Gita, he is also an efficient Tarot card reader, Astro-Vastu consultant, and a talented singer and composer. He has sung the entire Ram Charita Manas and Bhagavad Gita in his own compositions, and has sung the phrase "Lokah Samastha Sukhino Bhavantu" in 50 different languages. He is currently working on a detailed and scientific study of Vedas, Upanishads, Puranas, and the Bhagavad Gita. He has also composed and sung the Hanuman Chalisa and Gayatri Mantra in 108 and 1008 different compositions, respectively.

Awards - Four Times Guinness World Records, Winner of Mahatma Gandhi Vishwa Shanti Puraskar, Mahatma Gandhi Global Peace Ambassador, Kashi Ratna Award, Dr. APJ Abdul Kalam Motivational Person of the Year 2017, Mother Teresa Award, Indira Gandhi Priyadarshini Award, Bharat Vikas Ratna Award, Udyog Ratna Award, Vigyan Prasar Award, Poorvanchal Ratn Samman.

PREFACE

Tea drinking in India has a long and rich history, with tea having been consumed in the subcontinent for centuries. My goal for this book, The Indian Tea: A Cultural and Historical Overview of India's Tea Industry, is to explore the history and significance of India's tea industry and the many ways in which it has shaped Indian culture and society.

This book is intended to serve as an introduction to the rich history and culture of Indian tea for readers who are new to the subject. It explores the evolution of Indian tea from its traditional roots to its modern-day forms. The book covers various topics, including the development of different tea varieties, the influence of religion on Indian tea, and the impact of the Indian tea industry on the global market. It also examines the economics of Indian tea and the legacy of Indian tea in modern-day India.

The book draws on research from a variety of sources, including interviews with key figures in the Indian tea industry, archival materials, and cultural analysis. I have also conducted extensive field research in India, including attending tea ceremonies, interviewing tea producers, and visiting locations associated with the production of Indian tea. Through this research, I hope to provide readers with a comprehensive understanding of the Indian tea industry and its various components.

I am deeply passionate about the history and significance of Indian tea and hope that this book will help to spread the appreciation of this wonderful beverage. I believe that Indian tea has a great deal to offer to the world and I am excited to share its cultural and historical significance with my readers.

Normal Indian Tea With Milk

I

Introduction to the Indian Tea Industry

Introduction to the Indian Tea Industry

Tea is a staple beverage in India, with a rich history and cultural significance that has made it an integral part of the country's identity. India is the largest producer and consumer of tea in the world, and the Indian tea industry has a long and fascinating history that dates back to the mid-19th century. In this chapter, we will delve into the history of the Indian tea industry, its evolution over the years, and its impact on Indian society and the world at large.

The Origins of Tea Culture in India

Tea was first introduced to India by the British East India

Company in the mid-19th century. Initially, tea was cultivated in Assam, but it soon spread to other parts of the country, such as Darjeeling and Nilgiri. By the late 19th century, tea plantations were established across India, and the country had become a major player in the global tea trade.

The Growth of the Indian Tea Industry

The Indian tea industry continued to grow and expand throughout the 20th century, and by the mid-20th century, India had become the largest producer and exporter of tea in the world. The industry provided employment to millions of people, both on tea plantations and in tea-related industries, such as tea packaging and processing.

In the late 20th century, the Indian tea industry faced challenges, including declining tea prices, declining exports, and increasing competition from other countries. However, the industry continued to adapt and evolve, and today, India remains a major producer of tea, with a thriving industry that continues to grow and evolve.

The Impact of the Indian Tea Industry on Society

The Indian tea industry has had a profound impact on Indian society and the world at large. For example, the industry has provided employment to millions of people, helping to lift people out of poverty and improve their standard of living. The industry has also played a role in shaping the cultural and social identity of India, with tea being an integral part of the country's heritage and cultural traditions.

The Future of the Indian Tea Industry

The future of the Indian tea industry looks bright, with continued growth and expansion in the years to come. As the world's largest producer of tea, India will continue to play a major role in shaping the global tea market, and will continue to impact the lives of millions of people through its production and trade of this iconic beverage.

The Indian tea industry has a rich history and cultural significance that has shaped the country's identity and impacted the world at large. From its humble beginnings in the mid-19th century to its current status as the world's largest producer of tea, the Indian tea industry has grown and evolved to become an integral part of India's heritage and cultural traditions. As we delve deeper into the history of this iconic industry, we will gain a better understanding of its significance, both in India and around the world.

"Tea is not just a drink in India, it's a way of life steeped in history and tradition."

৪৩

II

History of Indian Tea

History of Indian Tea

The history of Indian tea dates back to the mid-19th century, when tea was first introduced to the country by the British East India Company. Since then, tea has become an integral part of Indian society and culture, with a rich and fascinating history that spans over a century and a half. In this chapter, we will explore the history of Indian tea, from its origins to the present day, and examine the cultural, social, and economic impacts that the tea industry has had on India and the world.

The Introduction of Tea to India

Tea was first introduced to India in the mid-19th century by the British East India Company. Initially, tea was grown in the Assam region of India, and it quickly spread to other parts of the country, such as Darjeeling and Nilgiri. By the late 19th century, tea plantations were established across India, and the country had become a major player in the global tea trade.

The Growth of the Indian Tea Industry

The Indian tea industry continued to grow and expand throughout the 20th century, and by the mid-20th century, India had become the largest producer and exporter of tea in the world. The industry provided employment to millions of people, both on tea plantations and in tea-related industries, such as tea packaging and processing.

In the late 20th century, the Indian tea industry faced challenges, including declining tea prices, declining exports, and increasing competition from other countries. However, the industry continued to adapt and evolve, and today, India remains a major producer of tea, with a thriving industry that continues to grow and evolve.

The Cultural Significance of Tea in India

Tea has a rich cultural significance in India, and has been an integral part of the country's heritage and cultural traditions for over a century. Tea is a staple beverage in India, and is consumed by people of all ages and walks of life. It is often served during special occasions and is an important part of Indian social gatherings.

The Impact of the Indian Tea Industry on Society

The Indian tea industry has had a profound impact on

Indian society and the world at large. For example, the industry has provided employment to millions of people, helping to lift people out of poverty and improve their standard of living. The industry has also played a role in shaping the cultural and social identity of India, with tea being an integral part of the country's heritage and cultural traditions.

The history of Indian tea is a rich and fascinating one, with roots that stretch back to the mid-19th century. The Indian tea industry has had a profound impact on Indian society and the world, providing employment to millions of people and shaping the cultural and social identity of India. Today, tea continues to be an important part of Indian society and culture, and the Indian tea industry remains a thriving and growing industry that continues to shape the world.

"Indian tea, with its unique blend of flavors
and aromas, has been captivating tea lovers
for centuries."

⊰⊱

III
Types of Indian Tea

Types of Indian Tea

India is home to a rich and diverse range of tea, each with its own unique flavor, aroma, and character. In this chapter, we will explore the various types of Indian tea, including their origin, production, and flavor profile.

Assam Tea

Assam tea is grown in the Assam region of India and is known for its bold, malty flavor. This type of tea is produced from the Camellia sinensis var. assamica plant, which is indigenous to the region. Assam tea is known for its strong flavor and is often used as the base for many tea blends, including chai.

Darjeeling Tea

Darjeeling tea is grown in the Darjeeling region of India and is known for its musky, floral flavor. This type of tea is produced from the Camellia sinensis var. sinensis plant, and is considered to be one of the finest teas in the world. Darjeeling tea is often referred to as the "champagne of teas" due to its unique flavor and aroma.

Nilgiri Tea

Nilgiri tea is grown in the Nilgiri region of India and is known for its light, floral flavor. This type of tea is produced from the Camellia sinensis var. sinensis plant, and is considered to be one of the finest teas in the world. Nilgiri tea is often used as the base for many tea blends, including green tea.

Chai Tea

Chai tea is a popular type of tea in India that is made from a blend of black tea, spices, and milk. Chai tea has a strong, spicy flavor and is often consumed in the morning or in the afternoon. Chai tea is an important part of Indian culture, and is often served during special occasions and social gatherings.

Green Tea

Green tea is a popular type of tea in India that is made from unfermented tea leaves. Green tea is known for its light, fresh flavor and is often consumed for its health benefits. Green tea is produced from the Camellia sinensis var. sinensis plant, and is considered to be one of the healthiest teas in the world.

India is home to a rich and diverse range of tea, each with its own unique flavor, aroma, and character. From the bold and malty flavor of Assam tea, to the musky and floral flavor of Darjeeling tea, and the light and fresh flavor of green tea, there is a type of tea for every taste and occasion. Whether you prefer a bold and flavorful tea or a light and fresh tea, India has something to offer everyone.

"From its humble beginnings, Indian tea has grown to become a thriving industry, defining the country's cultural and economic identity."

‰

IV

The Role of Religion in Indian Tea

The Role of Religion in Indian Tea

In India, tea has played an important role in the cultural and religious traditions of the country. From being used in Hindu religious rituals to serving as a symbol of hospitality in Islamic culture, tea has been intertwined with the spiritual beliefs of the Indian people for centuries. In this chapter, we will explore the role of religion in Indian tea culture.

Hinduism

In Hinduism, tea has played a role in religious rituals and offerings. For example, tea is often offered as a symbol of hospitality and respect when receiving guests or during temple offerings. In addition, tea is also commonly consumed by Hindu ascetics and yogis as a way to stay alert during meditation and other spiritual practices.

Islam

In Islamic culture, tea has long been associated with hospitality and generosity. When hosting guests, it is traditional to offer tea as a symbol of welcoming and comfort. Tea is also a common drink during Ramadan, the month of fasting, and is often consumed to break the fast in the evening.

Sikkhism

In Sikhism, tea holds a special significance as a symbol of unity and hospitality. Sikhs are encouraged to offer tea to guests as a sign of respect and kindness, regardless of their background or religion. Tea is also served as part of the Langar, a communal meal that is served in Sikh temples and is open to all people, regardless of their faith.

Buddhism

In Buddhism, tea is often consumed by monks and practitioners as a way to stay awake during meditation and other spiritual practices. Tea is also used in Buddhist tea ceremonies, which serve as a way to connect with the present moment and to cultivate mindfulness and inner peace.

Tea has played a significant role in the spiritual beliefs and cultural traditions of the Indian people for centuries. From being used in religious rituals to serving as a symbol of hospitality and unity, tea has been intertwined with the spiritual and cultural identity of India. Whether consumed as a symbol of respect, a tool for meditation, or a way to break the fast, tea remains an important part of the spiritual and cultural fabric of India.

"The journey of Indian tea from its origin to the global market has been a story of perseverance, innovation, and adaptation."

༄

V
Popular Indian Tea Varieties

Popular Indian Tea Varieties

India is the second-largest producer of tea in the world and is known for its diverse range of tea varieties, each with its unique flavor and aroma. From the bold and robust Assam tea to the delicate and fragrant Darjeeling tea, the Indian tea industry offers a vast selection of teas that cater to every taste preference. In this chapter, we will take a closer look at some of the most popular Indian tea varieties.

Assam Tea

Assam tea is one of the most popular tea varieties in India, known for its bold and malty flavor. This tea is grown in the Assam region of India, which is located in the northeastern part of the country. Assam tea is known for its high caffeine content and is commonly used in tea blends, including chai tea. This tea is also popular for its bright and full-bodied flavor, making it a great choice for those who prefer a strong and robust cup of tea.

Darjeeling Tea

Darjeeling tea is another popular Indian tea variety, known for its delicate and fragrant flavor. This tea is grown in the Darjeeling region of India, which is located in the eastern part of the country. Darjeeling tea is known for its floral and fruity aroma and is commonly referred to as the "champagne of teas". This tea is also popular for its light and delicate flavor, making it a great choice for those who prefer a delicate and nuanced cup of tea.

Nilgiri Tea

Nilgiri tea is a popular tea variety that is grown in the Nilgiri region of India, which is located in the southern part of the country. This tea is known for its crisp and clean flavor, which makes it a great choice for those who prefer a light and refreshing cup of tea. Nilgiri tea is also known for its bright and clear liquor, which makes it a great choice for those who prefer a clear and bright cup of tea.

Kangra Tea

Kangra tea is a popular tea variety that is grown in the Kangra region of India, which is located in the northwestern part of the country. This tea is known for its smooth and earthy flavor, which makes it a great choice for those who prefer a balanced and full-bodied cup of tea. Kangra tea is also known for its strong aroma, which makes it a great choice for those who prefer a fragrant and aromatic cup of tea.

The Indian tea industry offers a vast selection of teas that cater to every taste preference. From the bold and robust Assam tea to the delicate and fragrant Darjeeling tea, each tea variety has its unique flavor and aroma that make it a popular choice among tea drinkers. Whether you prefer a strong and robust cup of tea or a delicate and nuanced cup of tea, the Indian tea industry has something to offer for everyone.

"In India, tea is more than just a beverage, it's a symbol of hospitality, friendship, and community."

৪৩

VI

The Economics of Indian Tea

The Economics of Indian Tea

The tea industry in India plays a significant role in the country's economy, providing employment to millions of people and contributing to the country's Gross Domestic Product (GDP). In this chapter, we will take a closer look at the economics of the Indian tea industry, including its production, exports, and the factors that influence its growth and development.

Production and Exports

India is the second-largest producer of tea in the world, with an estimated annual production of over 1,400 million kilograms. The tea industry in India is largely dominated by small-scale farmers who own and operate tea gardens, as well as larger tea companies that own and operate multiple tea gardens. The tea produced in India is mainly exported to countries such as the United Kingdom, the United States, and Russia, among others.

Factors Influencing the Industry's Growth and Development

There are several factors that influence the growth and development of the Indian tea industry, including economic, political, and environmental factors. Economic factors such as changes in demand and supply, changes in consumer preferences, and fluctuations in the prices of tea can greatly impact the industry. Political factors, such as government policies and regulations, also play a significant role in the industry's growth and development. Environmental factors, such as climate change and the availability of natural resources, also play a significant role in the industry's success.

Challenges Faced by the Industry

Despite its significant contributions to the Indian economy, the tea industry in India faces several challenges that hinder its growth and development. Some of the key challenges faced by the industry include a lack of investment in research and development, limited access to markets, and limited access to financing for small-scale farmers. Additionally, the industry is also facing challenges related to climate change, such as unpredictable weather patterns and reduced water availability, which can impact the quality and yield of tea.

The tea industry in India plays a significant role in the

country's economy, providing employment to millions of people and contributing to the country's GDP. The industry is influenced by several economic, political, and environmental factors, as well as challenges related to climate change and limited access to financing. Despite these challenges, the tea industry in India continues to grow and develop, driven by the strong demand for its products and the commitment of its stakeholders to the industry's growth and success.

"The cultural significance of tea in India is evident in its rituals, customs, and traditions that have been passed down for generations."

৪৩

VII

Tea Cultivation and Production in India

Tea Cultivation and Production in India

Tea cultivation and production have been an integral part of India's history and culture for centuries. In this chapter, we will take a closer look at the process of tea cultivation and production in India, from planting to harvesting to processing and packaging.

Planting and Cultivation

Tea plants are propagated from cuttings or seeds, and the tea gardens in India are typically established on slopes or hillsides that receive sufficient sunlight and rainfall. The tea plants are pruned regularly to promote healthy growth, and the leaves are hand-picked to ensure the highest quality.

Harvesting

Tea harvesting in India typically begins in the spring and continues through the summer. The tea plants are harvested every 7 to 10 days, and the leaves are hand-picked by tea pluckers, who pick only the tender new leaves and buds. The leaves are then transported to the tea factory for processing.

Processing

The tea leaves undergo several stages of processing, including withering, rolling, oxidation, and drying. The withering process reduces the moisture content in the leaves, making them pliable for rolling. The rolling process helps to break down the cell walls in the leaves, which is necessary for oxidation. The oxidation process, also known as fermentation, is where the tea leaves take on their characteristic color and flavor. Finally, the dried leaves are sorted and packaged for sale.

Packaging and Exportation

The processed tea leaves are sorted according to their quality, size, and color, and then packaged for sale. The packaging process is carefully managed to ensure that the tea remains fresh and flavorful. India exports a significant portion of its tea production to countries around the world, and the country is renowned for its high-quality tea blends and single-estate teas.

Tea cultivation and production in India is a complex and multi-stage process that requires careful attention to detail and a commitment to quality. From planting to harvesting to processing and packaging, the tea industry in India is driven by the passion and dedication of its farmers and tea workers. The result is a rich and flavorful tea culture that has captured the hearts and palates of tea lovers around the world.

"Indian tea is known for its diversity, from
the bold and robust Assam tea to the delicate
and aromatic Darjeeling tea."

VIII

Indian Tea and the Global Market

Indian Tea and the Global Market

India is one of the largest producers and exporters of tea in the world, and the country's tea industry plays a significant role in the global tea market. In this chapter, we will explore the role of Indian tea in the global market and the factors that have made it such a popular and sought-after commodity.

Indian Tea and the Global Market

Indian tea has a long and rich history, and the country has been producing and exporting tea for over 150 years. Today, India is the second largest producer of tea in the world, and the country exports a significant portion of its tea production to countries around the world.

Factors Contributing to Indian Tea's Popularity

There are several factors that contribute to the popularity of Indian tea in the global market, including its rich and diverse flavor profiles, its high quality, and its competitive pricing. Indian tea is known for its rich and aromatic flavor, and the country produces a wide range of tea blends and single-estate teas, each with its own unique taste and character.

In addition to its flavor, Indian tea is also prized for its quality. The country has a well-established tea industry, and the tea gardens in India are held to strict quality standards. The tea plants are grown in ideal conditions, and the leaves are hand-picked to ensure the highest quality.

Finally, Indian tea is also competitively priced, making it accessible to tea lovers around the world. The country's large tea industry, combined with its favorable growing conditions, allows for cost-effective production, which is passed on to the consumer in the form of lower prices.

Challenges and Opportunities

While the Indian tea industry has been successful in the global market, there are still several challenges that the industry faces. One of the biggest challenges is competition from other tea-producing countries, such as China, Sri Lanka, and Kenya. These countries also produce high-quality tea, and they are vying for market share in the global tea market.

In addition to competition, the Indian tea industry is also

facing challenges related to labor, such as a shortage of skilled tea pluckers and an aging workforce. These challenges threaten the sustainability of the industry and the long-term viability of tea production in India.

Despite these challenges, the Indian tea industry is also filled with opportunities for growth and expansion. For example, there is a growing demand for specialty teas, such as organic and fair-trade teas, which offers new opportunities for growth in the Indian tea industry. Additionally, the increasing popularity of tea as a healthy beverage presents opportunities for the development of new tea products and new markets.

The Indian tea industry plays a significant role in the global tea market. With its rich and diverse flavor profiles, high quality, and competitive pricing, Indian tea is a popular and sought-after commodity. Despite facing challenges such as competition and labor issues, the Indian tea industry is also filled with opportunities for growth and expansion. Whether enjoyed as a daily beverage or as a special treat, Indian tea remains a beloved and iconic part of India's rich tea culture.

"Tea cultivation and production in India has been a source of livelihood for millions of farmers, creating a ripple effect on the country's economy."

⚭

IX

Indian Tea and the Global Market

Indian Tea and the Global Market

India is one of the largest producers and exporters of tea in the world, and the country's tea industry plays a significant role in the global tea market. In this chapter, we will explore the role of Indian tea in the global market and the factors that have made it such a popular and sought-after commodity.

Indian Tea and the Global Market

Indian tea has a long and rich history, and the country has been producing and exporting tea for over 150 years. Today, India is the second largest producer of tea in the world, and the country exports a significant portion of its tea production to countries around the world.

Factors Contributing to Indian Tea's Popularity

There are several factors that contribute to the popularity of Indian tea in the global market, including its rich and diverse flavor profiles, its high quality, and its competitive pricing. Indian tea is known for its rich and aromatic flavor, and the country produces a wide range of tea blends and single-estate teas, each with its own unique taste and character.

In addition to its flavor, Indian tea is also prized for its quality. The country has a well-established tea industry, and the tea gardens in India are held to strict quality standards. The tea plants are grown in ideal conditions, and the leaves are hand-picked to ensure the highest quality.

Finally, Indian tea is also competitively priced, making it accessible to tea lovers around the world. The country's large tea industry, combined with its favorable growing conditions, allows for cost-effective production, which is passed on to the consumer in the form of lower prices.

Challenges and Opportunities

While the Indian tea industry has been successful in the global market, there are still several challenges that the industry faces. One of the biggest challenges is competition from other tea-producing countries, such as China, Sri Lanka, and Kenya. These countries also produce high-quality tea, and they are vying for market share in the global tea market.

In addition to competition, the Indian tea industry is also

facing challenges related to labor, such as a shortage of skilled tea pluckers and an aging workforce. These challenges threaten the sustainability of the industry and the long-term viability of tea production in India.

Despite these challenges, the Indian tea industry is also filled with opportunities for growth and expansion. For example, there is a growing demand for specialty teas, such as organic and fair-trade teas, which offers new opportunities for growth in the Indian tea industry. Additionally, the increasing popularity of tea as a healthy beverage presents opportunities for the development of new tea products and new markets.

The Indian tea industry plays a significant role in the global tea market. With its rich and diverse flavor profiles, high quality, and competitive pricing, Indian tea is a popular and sought-after commodity. Despite facing challenges such as competition and labor issues, the Indian tea industry is also filled with opportunities for growth and expansion. Whether enjoyed as a daily beverage or as a special treat, Indian tea remains a beloved and iconic part of India's rich tea culture.

"The future of Indian tea is bright, as it continues to evolve and adapt to the changing demands of the global market while maintaining its traditional roots."

৪৩

X

The Impact of Indian Tea on Society

The Impact of Indian Tea on Society

The Indian tea industry has had a significant impact on society, both in India and around the world. In this chapter, we will explore the various ways that Indian tea has influenced society and the ways in which society has influenced the development of the tea industry in India.

The Economic Impact of Indian Tea

One of the most significant impacts of the Indian tea industry is its economic impact. The tea industry is a major source of employment in India, providing jobs for millions of people, from tea garden workers to tea merchants and traders. The industry also generates significant revenue for the country, both through the export of tea and through the sales of tea within India.

The tea industry has also played a role in the development of other industries in India, such as transportation and logistics. For example, the tea industry has been a driving force behind the development of India's railway system, which was originally built to transport tea from the gardens to the ports for export.

The Social Impact of Indian Tea

The Indian tea industry has also had a profound social impact, both in India and around the world. Tea has been an integral part of Indian society for centuries, and the tea culture in India is deeply rooted in the country's history and traditions. In India, tea is more than just a beverage - it is a symbol of hospitality and friendship, and it is an important part of daily life.

In addition to its social significance in India, Indian tea has also had a global impact on society. The popularity of Indian tea has contributed to the growth of tea culture around the world, and tea has become a staple beverage in many countries, from the United Kingdom to the United States. The global popularity of Indian tea has also helped to raise awareness about the rich cultural and historical significance of tea and its role in shaping societies around the world.

The Environmental Impact of Indian Tea

The Indian tea industry has also had an impact on the

environment, both positive and negative. On the one hand, tea gardens provide important habitats for wildlife and help to conserve the country's biodiversity. On the other hand, tea production can also have negative impacts on the environment, such as the use of harmful pesticides and the degradation of soil and water resources.

To address these environmental challenges, the Indian tea industry is working to adopt more sustainable practices, such as the use of organic and biodynamic methods of cultivation and the implementation of conservation programs to protect wildlife habitats.

The Indian tea industry has had a significant impact on society, both in India and around the world. From its economic impact to its social and environmental impact, Indian tea has shaped and been shaped by the societies in which it is produced and consumed. Whether enjoyed as a daily beverage or as a special treat, Indian tea remains an iconic and beloved part of India's rich tea culture, and its impact on society will continue to be felt for generations to come.

"In a world that's increasingly fast-paced,
Indian tea offers a moment of reflection and
connection with one's heritage and culture."

&

XI

The Future of Indian Tea

The Future of Indian Tea

As the world changes and evolves, the Indian tea industry is facing new challenges and opportunities. In this chapter, we will explore the future of the Indian tea industry, including trends and innovations that are shaping the industry, and the challenges that the industry must overcome to ensure its future success.

Trends and Innovations in Indian Tea

One of the key trends shaping the future of the Indian tea industry is the increasing demand for specialty and premium teas. As consumers become more discerning and seek out high-quality, unique tea experiences, the demand for specialty teas such as Darjeeling, Assam, and Nilgiri is on the rise. In response, the Indian tea industry is investing in research and development to create new and innovative tea blends and varieties that meet the demands of the global market.

Another trend shaping the future of the Indian tea industry is the increasing focus on sustainability and eco-friendliness. As consumers become more concerned about the environmental impact of the products they purchase, the tea industry is working to adopt more sustainable practices, such as organic and biodynamic cultivation methods, that minimize the industry's impact on the environment.

Finally, technology is also playing a major role in shaping the future of the Indian tea industry. From the use of drones to monitor tea gardens and improve yields, to the use of data analytics to optimize production and distribution, technology is helping to modernize the industry and improve its competitiveness in the global market.

Challenges Facing the Indian Tea Industry

Despite these positive trends and innovations, the Indian tea industry is facing a number of challenges that must be overcome to ensure its future success. One of the biggest challenges is the declining demand for tea in India, as consumers shift towards other beverages such as coffee and energy drinks. To address this challenge, the industry must find ways to re-energize the Indian tea market and promote tea as a healthy and appealing beverage choice.

Another challenge facing the Indian tea industry is the need to improve productivity and efficiency. With the rising costs of production and the increasing competition in the global market, the industry must find ways to streamline its operations and improve its competitiveness. This may involve investing in new technologies, improving agricultural practices, and exploring new markets for tea.

Finally, the Indian tea industry must also address the issue of labor rights and working conditions for tea garden workers. The industry has a responsibility to ensure that workers are treated fairly and given access to safe and healthy working conditions. To achieve this, the industry must work with government, labor organizations, and other stakeholders to implement fair labor practices and ensure the rights of workers are protected.

The future of the Indian tea industry is bright, with many exciting trends and innovations shaping the industry. However, to ensure its future success, the industry must overcome the challenges it faces, from declining demand to the need for improved productivity and efficiency. By embracing new technologies, promoting sustainability, and working to improve labor conditions, the Indian tea industry can continue to be a major player in the global market and an important part of India's rich tea culture.

"As the world continues to discover the treasures of Indian tea, its rich history, and cultural significance will continue to be celebrated for generations to come."

৪৩

Black Tea without Milk

OTHER BOOKS OF THE AUTHOR

1. The Moments When I Met God
2. Kashiyile Theertha Pathangal
3. GURU GYAN VANI
4. Abhiprerak Gita
5. ASSI SE JAIN GHAT TAK
6. Hopelessness of Arjuna
7. The Soul and It's True Nature
8. Sense of Action (Karma)
9. Action through Wisdom
10. Action through Wisdom
11. THEORY AND PRACTICAL OF EVERY ACTION
12. LOGICAL UNDERSTANDING OF THE SUPREME
13. THE IMPERISHABLE SUPREME
14. Yatra Nishadraj se Hanuman Ghat Tak
15. Yatra Karnatak Ghat se Raja Ghat Tak
16. Yatra Pandey Ghat se Prayagraj Ghat Tak
17. Yatra Ranjendra Prasad Ghat se Dattatreya Ghat Tak
18. YaatraSindhiya Ghat se Gwaliar Ghat Tak
19. Yatra Mangala Gauri Ghat se Hanuman Gadhi Ghat Tak
20. Yatra Gaay Ghat Se Nishad Ghat Tak
21. MAA GANGA, GHATEN EVM UTSAV
22. Ganga Arti Dev Deepavali evam Any Utsav
23. Potentials of Digitalized India
24. VEDIC CONSCIOUSNESS
25. A Brief Introduction to Vedic Science
26. Kashi ke Barah Jyotirling
27. IMPACT OF MOTIVATION
28. Let's have a Milky Way Journey
29. Color Therapy in a Nutshell

30. Rigveda in a Nutshell
31. Yajurveda in a Nutshell
32. Samveda in a Nutshell
33. Atharva Veda in a Nutshell
34. Ayushman Bhava - Ayurveda
35. Srimad Bhagavad Gita and Upanishad Connection
36. Srimad Bhagavad Gita - an attempt to summarize each chapter.
37. Facts and Impact of Nakshatra
38. Astro Gems - NAVARATNA
39. Ekadashi - A Concise Overview
40. A Concise View of Hanuman Chalisa
41. Inspirational Gita
42. Nakshatraranyam
43. Summary of 18 Mahapuranas
44. Synopsis of 18 Upa Puranas
45. Rigvediya Upanishads
46. Shukla Yajurvediya Upanishads
47. Krishna Yajurvediya Upanishads
48. Samavediya Upanishads
49. Atharvavediya Upanishads
50. The Seven Great Sages
51. From Rocket Scientist to President Dr. APJ Abdul Kalam
52. The Visionary's Voice - Quotes of Dr. APJ Abdul Kalam
53. The Wisdom of Swami Vivekananda: Insights and Inspiration from a Legendary Spiritual Teacher
54. Ayurvedic Remedies from the Garden
55. Sages and Seers
56. Rising Strong – Motivational Stories of Women
57. Beyond Flames -Mystery stories of Funeral Ghat Manikarnika
58. The Origins of Tulsi: A Look at the Mythological Roots of the Plant"

59. The Holistic Cow: A Look at the Physical, Spiritual, and Cultural Importance of Cows in India
60. Arts of Healing
61. Exploring the Divine
62. Understanding Five Elements
63. The Etymology of Ram
64. Symbols of India
65. Voice of Change (About Speeches of Great Men)
66. She Speaks (About Speeches of Great Women)
67. Patriotism on Celluloid – Brief About Patriotic Films
68. The Music of Motivation: A Brief Guide to Inspirational Film Songs
69. **Unlocking the Secrets of the Dashopanishads**
70. A Cultural Mosaic
71. Ancient Traditions, Modern Minds
72. Ecos of Ancient Wisdom
73. Beneath the Surface
74. From Temples to Ashrams
75. Sages of the Subcontinent
76. The Art of Healling (Ayurveda, Yoga & Naturopathy)
77. Indian Kitchen
78. The Festivals of India
79. The Indian Epics Retold
80. The Power of Mantras
81. The Indian River Ganges
82. The Indian Architecture
83. Rites of Passage
84. The Indian Silk Road
85. The Indian Literature
86. The Indian Villages
87. The Indian Folks & Crafts
88. The Way of Buddha
89. The Ramayan of Tulsidas

121. Innovative Startups - 25 Startup Ideas to Spark Your Business Creativity
122. Export Management: Strategies for Global Success
123. Exporting from India - A Step by Step Guide
124. Finance Fundamentals: Mastering Financial Management for Business Success
125. Global Growth Strategies for International Business Development
126. Marketing Mastery: Unlocking the Secrets of Modern Marketing
127. Operations Mastery: Managing the Flow of Value in Business
128. Strategic Business Management: Navigating the Modern Business Landscape
129. Human Resource Management Strategies for Building and Managing a High Performance Team
130. The Indian Landscapes and Nature: An Exploration Of India's Natural Beauty And Diversity
131. The Indian Street Performances: A Cultural Exploration of India's Street Performances
132. Affirming Your Self-Worth: Strategies for Achieving Emotional Wellbeing
133. Cultivating Self-Discipline: Secrets Methods for Achieving Your Goals
134. Embracing Change: Strategies for Adapting to Life's Challenges
135. Embracing Your Uniqueness: Secret Strategies for Living an Authentic Life
136. Finding Motivation in Despondency: Coping with Difficult Times
137. Embracing Change
138. Learning to Love Yourself
139. Managing Time for Yourself

৪৩

CONTACT

DR. JAGADEESH PILLAI

MBA & PhD in Vedic Science

Four Times Guinness World Record Holder

Winner of Mahatma Gandhi Vishwa Shanti Puraskar and
Global Peace Ambassador

Gemology, Astro & Vastu Consultant - Spiritual Counselor

Consultant for designing World Record Ideas

Efficient Tarot Card Reader

9839093003

myrichindia@gmail.com

drjagadeeshpillai@facebook

drjagadeeshpillai@instagram
jagadeeshpillai@youtube

www. JAGADEESHPILLAI.com

ೞ

|| LOKAHA SAMASTHAHA SUKHINO BHAVANTU ||

www.ingramcontent.com/pod-product-compliance
Lightning Source LLC
Chambersburg PA
CBHW031358160726
47993CB00003B/1026